Night School: Selected Early Poems

by

Glen Armstrong

ISBN: 978-93-95224-14-7

First Edition: 2022
Rs. 200/-

Cyberwit.net
HIG 45 Kaushambi Kunj, Kalindipuram
Allahabad - 211011 (U.P.) India
http://www.cyberwit.net
Tel: +(91) 9415091004
E-mail: info@cyberwit.net

Printed at VCORE LLP.

. . . we have entered an illegal time, a night beyond control,
liable to all kinds of excesses and crazes.

Bruno Schulz

It's not too far back off the highway, not so long a ride.

Chuck Berry

Contents

I.

Never Quite Coming of Age in Pontiac Michigan

It's never too late
to enjoy the information age.
But first,
there might be a bird in the basement.

There might be a hole in the house
where the birds get in.

I have been warned often enough
of the chimney and our home's
state of disrepair.

There are discoveries to be made
on cable television,
countless programs on birds and home improvement.

A bird's wing houses over 10,000 bones.
I wish that I had 10,000 bones.

A bird gets up early in the morning.
It catches the worm, and the worm becomes it.

Or it leaves the nest
to stick in the neck of a cat like a bone,
a sharp and slender bone.

All of my wishes are wrong.

The north wind blows
several birds from the sky.

It's best that I stay inside.
My conclusions are all wrong,
as are the few decisions that I make

out of feathers.
Horse feathers.
I love that one.

It must be wrong to love that one
when the wind blows
and I have no other way

to be inside, just a bit
more inside than I already am.

If someone could show me how to compose
a protest song, it would go like this:

When we were children, even inside
our mothers, we knew nothing
real existed inside the television.

This is a comfort; this is an empty box
I will someday inherit.

Creation Theory

You came from a caveman.
You came from an egg.
You came from a stork.
You came from a limousine.
The caveman hunted the stork.
Your mother applied orange makeup to her body.
You didn't begin at the beginning.
Your father held the door.
Her gown swallowed the red rose.
You weren't the first to hunger.
You came from the museum of natural history.
You were the apple.
The gears spun their partners around.
You were captivated
by the ape-man diagram.
You were the planet's rotation.
You were your father's eye.
You flew with the angels
through the lens you had been.
And when you came home from the hospital,
and when the tectonic plates shifted,
and when the star of Bethlehem
appeared seven times brighter than anything
the hunter-gatherers had seen at night,
we fed you cookies
and nicknamed you "turtle shell."
You poked your head out of yourself.

Consider how cold and theoretical one straight line
starting arbitrarily and pushing toward infinity seems.
When I dream of you, some unknown character
opens a bottle of toenail polish,
and the smell wakes me up
from my beautiful but desperate thoughts,
from the protean yoke and yellow protein,
from the wings that dreamers wear,
from the wheels against the planet's bare skin.
In the beginning, before the darkness,
there were at least three words.

Breakfast Meditation

The sunrise rejuvenates our maple tree
with an eerie, green halo

so beautifully.
It breaks my heart.

Another day is dawning,
time's marvelous inchworm outwitting
civilization's greatest evil geniuses:

Victor Frankenstein,
undefended at his trial by torch
and lynch mob,

the Marquis de Sade with no one
to talk to after the orgy.

All crimes against nature
are merely failures to communicate.

I want to discuss magic and sorrow.
The newspaper discusses arson

on the front page,
but later on

it briefly discusses Sagittarians,
those passionate misfits
born to a fire sign in the middle of winter.

There are planets in my house,
and my heart has chambers.

It's as dangerous to keep repeating mistakes
as it is to mistake repetition
as the villain of this little story.

Little by little, stroke by stroke.

I've poured you some coffee.

Measuring the marigolds.

Famous Succubus Trading Cards

Through burning piles of leaves,
past the Doberman house –
there was a tree; there would be other trees –
we cut back through the alley on our bikes
and turned on Chilton Boulevard.

Birds turning into bats, particles of light
bending under twilight's pressure.
There were several items on our agenda:

I liked the way gravel made a broken sound
caught up in the spokes; she liked the stars
and striped pants older girls wore.

I thought her red reflectors
made the back of her bike look like dragon eyes;
she thought her dad might know
what we'd done to his hot lather maker.

I had the torn corner off a black light poster,
some of the pink vibrating lines
rising up to pollute a shirtless couple;
she had several packs
of Famous Succubus Trading Cards
and some good ones at that.

Into a ditch and out again,
cutting through behind the drug store
and up hill from there,

I arrived at our secret meeting place
knowing whatever I offered her wouldn't be enough.

For the first time, I was holding her hand
more than she was holding mine.

Night School Fight Song

We are proud of our school.
We are true.

When we spray-paint the names
of our favorite rock bands
on the auditorium,
we try to stay between the lines.

Our hours are bigger than yours.
This winter semester will never contain us.

We are to this classroom
as December is to snowflake.

We remember things
by imagining
things that never happened:

Last Tuesday night a stoned Eskimo
appeared near the window sparking his Zippo.

It's not that we lose interest.
It's not that we're slow.

We are here because we can't think straight
in the daylight
where nothing seems

like anything
but what it is.

Chief Pontiac Answers Lord Jeffrey Amherst

I understand that your piece of parchment
is an act of war,

that the little sticks you've scattered upon it
are a type of language.

You would like me to stop attacking forts;
that is the gist of this dirty flag.

But tell me, Son of Amherst,
who of your people conceived this communication

broken into little slash marks?
How do voices reach your gods

snapped apart and imprisoned in such a way?
How can they mix with the clouds?

We will fight, and I might lose,
but allow me this prophecy:

one-hundred years from now
your name will mark a valley of death,

a people perpetually mourning.
Your mightiest medicine woman will hide from you,

her broken incantations never whispered aloud,
but set like beaver traps

that will drive your gifted daughters mad
for countless generations.

Our Finest Hour: July 20, 1969

1.

The astronauts are doing it.
Man is walking on the moon.

This is no rumor.
All of the hearsay is here

in my backyard doing the mambo
with someone else's wife.

The babies have crashed,
but no one makes me go to bed.

I no longer fear my parents'
drunken speculations:

Armstrong's weird boot
will silently crunch the moon

and all hell will break loose.
The satellite will crumble

underneath him, changing the way
we think about the sky.

I am a child too young to appreciate
the history being made,

as if against its will,
to settle down into a moment.

2.

I usually like to be around adults,
but tonight my aunts and uncles

are moving like broken toys.
My parents' friends are picking up

sides as if for kickball
or a street fight.

I am talking to myself
but listening to a stranger

sob near the wading pool
full of beer and ice.

He says he can't find the whiskey.
He can't quite grasp

my shirt sleeve as he says,
"Hey kid, this is all a big mistake."

No one shoos me away.
He can't shoo the fat black hornet

from his cheek as he murmurs,
". . . drop the big one. . ."

then damns Nostradamus
and curses Doris Day.

Night presses hard into his face
between these last cohesions.

He is breaking up,
all communication lost.

I don't want to be an astronaut.
If I have to grow up,

I'd rather, for a living,
be an archeologist,

reading the bones
of superstitious primitives

trapped in the volcanic ash of Pompeii
or the burned-out back yards of suburbia.

Meditation on a Tool and Die Shop, 40 Miles North of Detroit

1.

The "Big Green" is a "Cincinnati."
The "Cincinnati" is a horizontal milling machine.

It sprays metal shavings all over the place,
then needs to cool down.

Shipments of steel arrive.
Day in, day out,
the bars enter big and leave in pieces.

Today, the industrial drums are filling up
with modified 2 x 5/8 table clamps.

Once cut to size, drilled and tapped,
these clamps are stamped left hand or right.

A system is needed.

An accurate count.

A smoother finish.

2.

In the welding booth, intense flame
makes even thick material
transparent.

In January, weldments harden
in the courtyard snow,
melting their own peculiar shapes
into the green and dirty brown
beneath white winter.

In mid-June, open doors reveal
some of what happens
in this strangely engaging building

visible from the highway.

Light, like all radiation,
becomes less threatening
with distance.

3.

I love the tool and die industry,
how it easily blends into that great horizon
like a song in the public domain.

Let clouds be clouds.

The clang of metal against bigger metal,
better metal.

A hand completely dedicated
        to its craft continues working

        as if nothing worthwhile
        will ever again be made of wood.

Mr. and Mrs. Tattoo

We each got a tattoo
to prove that we love each other.

Soon, we each got a second tattoo
to prove that we really wanted the first.

The third tattoo commemorated
something too painful to talk about.

People would constantly ask
about the third tattoo

so we covered it
with the fourth tattoo.

The fifth tattoo just appeared
as if inked by elves in the night.

Each tattoo had a special meaning
except the sixth tattoo.

The seventh tattoo continued a story
about a mermaid and a sailor

and an endlessly indifferent shoulder blade.
The eighth tattoo

was carefully planned
but secretly, a disappointment.

There were so many more.
Some of them tried to connect

back to that first tattoo.
They wanted to be part of a single covering,

to always answer the question
"how many?"

with "one."
Others wanted their place on our bodies

to be theirs and theirs alone.
They resented any repetition

of color or line.
We became a sort of buzz around town,

a sighting in the supermarket
or furniture store.

Children were told not to stare
and told if they didn't forget the glimpse

they got of us that the impulse
to cover their flesh in pictures

would just erupt someday.
They would have to get jobs in circuses

or doing data entry from home.
We learned to smile and nod at our curious

but sometimes frightened neighbors.
And thus we grew old

sipping Earl Gray tea on the back porch
of our farm house, increasingly

confused about what to do
with our hands, our eyelids,

our genitals.
It is sometimes hard to see

any natural conclusion
or to remember that this business

with all its twists and turns
started as an act of love.

Reenactment

I am the only one
devoted to war's quieter moments:

Misheard whisperings of spies.
Sideways glances before the siege.

I replaced that plank in the Trojan horse's ass
while Agamemnon's army slept.

No one knows me.

While blue and grey face off
amid choreographed cannon smoke.

While the bugle blares.
While the drum and fife serenade
the bloodless.

While history applauds
its own imperfect reflection.

I am the conscientious objector
sweeping the V. A. asylum's floor
clean enough for poetry.

The caged clock.

The night nurse.

The suicide.

II.

Black Coffee

Do I want room for cream?
No. I order my coffee black,
“black as death,”

which isn’t funny,
especially when the three washed-out punks
to my left start chanting:

“I love coffee. I love espresso. I love death...”
which sounds familiar, but instead
of realizing that they’re mocking me,

I assume they’re quoting Black Flag,
or maybe Nietzsche, and it’s true
that they’re slamming double espressos

with a jittery, loose-bolt gusto.
They’re quoting the black holes in their mugs.
They’re quoting a pack of wolves.

They’re quoting the half-naked beggar
who asks for immortality
but accepts a handful of change.

They are mocking life’s oddness
and darkness and clever old farts
who only find solace in the words of tin gods.

Political Poem for Garrison Keillor

If no one is conquering evil,
    I give up.
If no one is showing his rosebud or doodlebug to the devil,
    I'll at least stand vigil

    between the entrance of the 7-11
    and its dark green dumpster.

Every now and then a chicken is born
    with a human face,

    a bicycle thief leaves a smear of chocolate frosting
    on the rusty hacksaw blade,

    dinner never makes it to the table.
    We all sit in the parlor until three a.m.
    wishing we had a machine
    to make something useful out of our voices.

If I'm not talking,
    it's not that I don't know what Virge did to Lucinda
    last Halloween after the hayride.
If I'm not talking,
    it's not that I'm embarrassed about the gold tooth
    Doc Stannard hooked me up with
    after the root canal.
If I'm not talking,
    it's not that I'm not plotting revenge

or whispering angry love poems in a voice so soft
and deep that it merely massages my gums.

The farmers never eat a chicken like that,
and they never let it reproduce.

It lives out its life in a separate coop.
Children ask it questions.

A tooth like that is worth more than gold.
It's neither legal nor tender.

Flowers in Stone

after Paul Klee

Though hardly a blockhead,
he only had twelve thoughts
in heavy rotation in that radio

station of a head of his:
Lily's round bottom,
birds caught in a wind storm

and ten other ordinary things
modified by nine deep feelings.
This was enough for an ever-

changing picture, an infinite melody,
and when Klee lay down
at night, a swarm of philosophical

fireflies flocked to one thing
or another, burning rhythm
and beauty into the blossoms

collected by day: petals break
stone by becoming stone.
Stone catches fire; stone learns to fly.

Diner Coated in Such a Fine Layer of Death That Nobody Notices

The governor vetoed all funding.
    And the newscaster slurred her words.

Robbie and Tim made coleslaw
    at the Peppermill Café,

    then a Nike ad announced very little
    with the conviction
    of the swords
    of a thousand men.

It was nearly Groundhog's Day.
    One of the old timers predicted

    that we'd never see another woman
    pop out of a cake.

With no more passion
    than it would take to let air out of a tire,

    we ate our lunch.
        Odysseus killed monsters.

    A K-9 unit pulled into the lot.
        We hardly noticed

        the slow, deliberate strokes
        waiting off to the side

like a bone yard
or a tabloid magazine.

We never saw the television's hands.
A cabbage has no throat.

Androgynous

Androgynous as rubber bands,
we kissed in the optometrist's dumpster.

We stumbled from each other's lips,
then went off into the night.

We liked the numbers above doorways
and the way weeds would crack cement

eventually. When we peed in the abandoned
parking lot, she turned into a rubber duck,

but I turned into nothing.
It was scary and weirdly calming

to be nothing.
Across town, the cheerleaders

and football captains broke curfew
under the water tower,

naked as ax handles.
To them, we were less than nothing

in our mascara and Mission of Burma tee-shirts.
It was all about camouflage . . .

or being seen. I forget.
For one glorious summer, we were mirrors

pressed together, nothing but shiny green edges
and black paper to the world.

City of Hats

It's not a city of secrets.
Whenever couples meet the buildings tip.

When they make love
the windows fly across the sky.

Stairways spiral down around necks
like beautiful scarves.

Turbans unravel.
Travelers can never find their rooms.

The rats eat the birds
and the hats eat the rats.

The doorways are full of black velvet
and broken cowboy boots.

There was an ill-advised dual here
fought between the night

and the naked person in my hat.
There will be trouble here again tomorrow,

young fedoras on the beaches,
the smell of hair spray waiting at the rim.

It’s a city only debutantes
and balding men believe in.

It’s a city in the end,
just a little bigger than my head.

How the Blind Man Gets Home from the Bar

Like a train, he simply runs on time,
the beer and the whiskey a rhythm,
the chaos at home
a clockwork.

What one prehistoric weed
confesses to another under pressure.

When the florist severs the stem of a rose,
she knows her way back to Eden.

The blind man with a lump of coal
will find the nearest furnace.

Or so I've heard the poet argue with the priest.

When he holds a length of wire,
he can follow it back to the porch light.

When he holds the length of pipe,
he can follow it back to the kitchen sink.

After last call, he takes hold of his broken shovel,
shoveling coal, shoveling coal,

feeding the dark stuff he's become
to the night's weary engine.

The Girl Who Liked Scary Movies

She was seven when I was twelve.
She was clever when I was water.
She took baths when I took showers.
She was X when I was the Science Patrol.
Her green Crayola was the one she loved best,
the one that ran away from her the quickest.
Godzilla was green and Frankenstein
and most of the rest of what she drew
had a jagged green outline to signify
the otherworldly:

A top-hatted granddad
with a knife and one eye.
An undead parakeet.
An army of radioactive boyfriends.

She told me that she had eleven daddies
when she was little,
but that her real daddy
was moving back home . . .
even though he accidentally killed a turtle.
She was drawing a green lightning bolt
when I was drawing a map to the treasure.
"But that's a secret I'm not supposed to tell,"
she said, shaking her green crayon at me.

We didn't see each other for years.
She was exploding when I was driving.
She was developing a reputation when I was an anarchist.

She was combing her hair when I was asleep.
She was mentioned when I was listening.
And though I still haven't seen her
since she lived down the street,
I dreamed of her last night:

She was quietly raising her daughter,
while I was a forensic detective,
reprimanded by the chief for outlining
the bodies with green chalk
instead of the approved tombstone white.

And in that Silly-Putty place
between dream and daylight,
I was in love with her for a moment.
Though she never recognized me
as she searched for quarters in her purse,
I was lurching toward her
from an entirely different world.

American Poet in Tokyo

I was ill-equipped for Japan.
My box full of weird little lyrics
didn't really translate,

so I worked the crowd.
I learned to be their American,
as huge and unruly

as they hoped I would be,
the English I taught them only
good for starting fist fights

or seducing those already confused.
There were sightings. I was spotted
through the city like jazz or a buffalo.

I smiled only when Kaoko
offered me a strawberry confection.
No one panicked.

No one took me or the candy
or the ten-thousand blinking
neon signs seriously.

Everywhere I looked,
young couples ate pink
mystery-discs from little packages,

each box decorated
with a different geometric mammal
and its otherworldly love song.

Chicken

Consider the novelty of a chicken
on a city sidewalk.

Two boys -- too young for girls,
too old for toys – kill the chicken.

They kick and stomp the meatiest pieces
into the concrete, into a flatline salad.

They stain the walkway, tossing
its bones and twisting its head.

They break its beak
and dissolve its shiny black eyes.

Consider their steel-toed boots,
the unbearable newness,

their mannish feet settling
for novelty: death, a shiny penny.

They walk away as the feathers settle
and never look back.

The boys do not understand
the purpose of a chicken.

III.

The Joys of Poetry

All things are probable.
All things turn into a cherry.

A beautiful woman touching her tooth.

Chief Pontiac Digs His Fortress of Solitude

I am digging a hole
and wearing my Sunday best.

I am digging a deeper hole
and have given my earthly possessions away.

I am hoping to strike not treasure but time,
for I desperately need to do some thinking.

But I am never quite sure
if the shovel is striking time or not.

It might be like striking a clock
or a clock striking itself

or a clock striking time
or rather one of time's hours.

My shovel strikes the occasional rock
which pleases me,

infinity in all the local folklore
depicted as littered with rocks.

My wife throws a rock at my head,
for she knows that I'm a man

of infinite potential
but a tragic passion for digging.

She gathers the children around,
and soon the neighbors are peeking

over our shoulders.
Soon she is begging me to stop

as the curious crowd starts singing
"Stairway to Heaven," holding hands,

swaying, circling around me
and calling their nearest neighbors

on their cell phones to come join in.
Though I promise my wife that I'm not digging

my grave but my secret laboratory,
the widows offer her handkerchiefs.

A handsome younger warrior offers my sons
sticky, lint-covered Tic Tacs

from his pocket and watches
to see if my wife notices his kindness.

The impromptu serenade starts to fall apart
as one of my neighbors sings,

just a bit too loudly
and a bit too beautifully,

"If there's a hedgehog in your bedroll,
don't be alarmed now,"

and a newer voice to the chorus
insists that the correct lyric is,

"If there is headroom in your Rolex
don't be alarmed now."

Fist fights break out over the words.
My children start to cry.

It's getting harder and harder
to find a place to think in this town.

Centennial

The flower, bird and flag prove nothing.
Anything can flutter in the wind.

But what of the rock, Grandfather?

The pencil lead unsteady in its socket,
the felt pens dry,
the old man searches the cabin
for something that leaves a mark.

He is the darker of the grandfathers,
the one who always has rolls of butcher paper
to draw on, the mentor of myth and banner.

So our drawings of rocks and rock formations
start in our minds and end up vulnerable
to the physical world?

We will be rock people, Boy, but not forever.
I like a flag in the dark
and a tattered flag
and a flag that the owls shit on.

There's an anthem here somewhere,
in a drawer if I'm not mistaken.

Instead of Discussing Marriage

I should have opened the window
    to yell at stray dogs,

slunk from the bed like a wounded satyr,

thoroughly checked her naked body
    for anything the gray men
    from outer space might have implanted,

offered to fix her breakfast,

tried to explain the family curse
    that held me honor-bound
    to name my firstborn "Tuesday,"

compared her to a summer day:
    her pirate tattoo a patch of fresh asphalt,
    her breasts competing ice cream trucks,

had her explain to me again the difference
    between films and movies,

assured her that it wasn't her but me,

insisted that I never discuss
    such life-changing events without first
    consulting Mom and L. Ron Hubbard,

had her define "marriage" in 1,200 words or less,

refused to discuss such options
until our gay and lesbian brothers and sisters
were granted the right to do the same,

asked her to make me breakfast,

demanded that she ask me the price
of grapefruit, *en français*,

urged her to live in the moment,

urged her to live in the urge,

urged her to live with me out of wedlock
in a one room shack,

asked if her stepmother had sent the green
ceramic kitten from Tokyo,

predicted that heartbreak would once again
change the face of contemporary poetry,

sung all twelve verses of "American Pie"
into her hairbrush,

argued that a salmon's spawning ritual,
not the actual spawning, doomed it,

remembered what Emerson wrote:
there is no luck nor witchcraft
nor destiny nor dignity
in marriage,

started planning a trip to the beehive state,

massaged the small of her back,

drawn a map on the bed sheet
with a purple felt-tip pen,
a wedding arch and gazebo,

an x to mark how far we were
from there,

put *Too Much Too Soon* by the New York Dolls
on the turntable,

questioned that sliver of primordial light
shot like an arrow
lodged in her heart,

propelled from the big bang's center
at a pace I could never keep up with.

I should have been more honest,
more deceitful,

more chivalrous
or more of a perfect rogue,

but we were young and I wanted her
to float from the bed
with the same radiant faith in me
that had undressed her
and put her there in the first place.

King Lear

1.

Lear was a man of the world.
Lear was a Lear Jet entering
a triangle worse than Bermuda,
a nude, outdated jet adrift
in an atonal symphony
of guts and ham sandwiches.

The world wants our insides back.
The planet only wants our skin.

2.

When I was six my sister rubbed
a dandelion on my forehead.
I was yellow
which meant that I secretly loved girls.
The flower was smeared with dead skin cells
which meant I was falling apart.
My shoe was untied.
Every time I tried to say my abc's
the l-m-n-o-p bunched up like a bully's fist.
I gave my sister a punch on the arm
and the wild finches scattered.
Finch on the telephone line.
Finch in the tomcat's mouth.
Soft finch adrift in the wind x ten.
Whispering finch in my head x the yellow-grey
of a summer storm.

Year of the Rabbit

Talented and affectionate,
you are the luckiest of all signs.

You could sit all day
in the China Jade's red vinyl booths

collecting woo from the place mat
completely without incident.

You are younger than some and older
than others: year of the rooster, year of the cat.

The speckled shark in the fish tank
hasn't got a year.

A student of Bakelite Buddhas,
alone with your bowl of hot and sour soup,

you dream of the younger waitress
with her long black hair tied up in chopsticks.

You anticipate the heat of her kisses
with each spoonful you slurp.

This is enough.
You eat your soup

as if no one and nothing
was ever bred for brevity or decoration.

Muskrat

"Sometimes our friendship feels
like a stack of rare, overdue library books
left to yellow in a hollow tree.

Sometimes I think you'd be the perfect
man to fall in love with . . ."
Sometimes I think about calling her bluff

by tracing my name on her arm
with a gentle but committed fingertip.
More often, we spend the afternoons

sipping coffee we can't quite afford
and debating whether or not
famous poets imitate animals as they work.

She has glands in her ankles
that secrete a strange perfume,
and the Braille of her goose flesh

never says "sometimes."
Sometimes I think that if the animals
had a language, the goose and the muskrat

would forego verse altogether,
neither willing to let poetry kill off
appetite in endless conversation.

Garage Band

They are closer to the garden hose
    than Hendrix.

The bag of rusty hammers
    hanging near the drummer's head

    suggests they call the band
    Thunder God,

but the quiet boy
    on rhythm guitar,
        who secretly gets good grades,
    suggests

    The Ball Turret Gunners.

They all agree at least
    that the band's name
    should seem to fall from above:

  Sky Captains of Today

        Rain of Terror

            Angel Sperm

They know that as soon as the perfect
    name is uttered aloud,

naked girls will be passing
it through their lips.

They're all sure of this

except for the quiet boy
who knows too well how the best words
tend to end up stillborn.

God Is Dude

He is drag racing the moon to Phoenix Arizona
fueled by nothing but a fifth of Jack Daniel's.

He is playing the lead in a play based on a song
about a playwright who sings songs
but secretly wants to act in a play
based on someone else's song.

He is angry at his absent father
but fascinated by beatniks.

He always says,
"a gun for protection is worth an ounce of prevention."

All of the coins in his basement safe are buffalo nickels.
All of the comic books under his bed are *Action Comics* #1.

He floats like a butterfly but stings like a sunburn.

He knows from experience that there are no fish
in Palookaville, only fishermen.

He doesn't insist that everything pressing
her black cocktail dress from its flat existence is heart.

The sooner He gets started, the harder they fall.

He maintains an interest in Dixieland jazz.
He played the trombone at Nietzsche's funeral.

My sister found Him once after her second abusive marriage.
He was sad but clean shaven.
The waitresses all called him, "Sir," except for Lishba,
who was Hindu and referred to him as "Tex."

We are His children and His prison.
He can never leave for a three day weekend.

He sometimes likes to sit on the porch
imagining things he's never seen before,
a chess piece wearing a see-through blouse,
for example.

Once, during the Crimean War,
He battled a whole platoon of Russian soldiers
single-handedly, high on the cliffs of Telegraph Hill.
The roar of the Alma below muffled
His catlike execution of Judo chops,
Kung-fu kicks and lethal Aikido throws.
It was as if a ghost wearing brass knuckles
had gone berserk amid these men
who, moments earlier, were boasting of all
the despicable things they would do
for a steak and the company of a woman.
Maybe it's His wrath, maybe His justice,
but one by one the Russians fall,
rib fragments driven into hearts,
spines traumatized where fragile necks bloom into skulls.
One moment, the head is a thing with a face,
full of dreams, full of plans
to open a French-style bistro back home
after all this ugly business is finished.
The next, the soldier's head is a collapsing vegetable,

a pumpkin emptied by something it never
much believed in in the first place.

Remember, this is war.

He is always there.
When you are taking a bubble bath
after an overtime shift at the cannery,
He will barge through the door
knocking over one of the scented candles
you have lit to magically ward off such intrusions.
He needs to confess that though He loves you best,
He loves an entire planet of women.
You half suspect that He loves most of the men as well.
He displays more confusion than remorse.
He distractedly wonders what the two of you
should do about dinner.

And you'll have to forgive Him.
After all, He has already forgiven you.

Dandelion

Like anything else
that starts with a kiss
the wind, sometimes violent

sometimes barely there at all,
jiggles the weeds and the willows.
Nothing scatters.

Like anything else
that refuses to scatter,
the dandelion is young

and hasn't yet seen its own undoing
in the fractured husk of a seed.
It needs no mythology

to feel the sun
or brave the wind or live
as a citizen in a yellow metropolis.

The sun is now.

It sees, instead, immortality,
a mint-condition forever.
The dandelion knows nothing

ever failed to jump
fully grown and cricket-quick
from its own fragile skull.

IV.

As Her Children Debate Godzilla's Gender

I try to taste my own mouth.
Daddy's breath weapon.
Mommy's path of destruction.

I'm neither Mommy nor Daddy,
just the date:
love's adjunct faculty,

a bat their mother won't shoo from the room,
foreign wings that darken the sky
and put the doll house up for sale.

Godzilla, they conclude, is simply Godzilla.
An aberrant force of nature.
Nothing but fang and tail.

Its eggs are not its own.
There's no reason they should love it.
By the end of the night

it will have returned to its home
on Monster Island, though less of a threat,
its mysterious sex still glowing.

Disclaimer for Disney's *Pinocchio*: February 1940

There will be colors, shapes and Italy.
For a while, at least,
all will go horribly wrong.

The floors will be sticky.
The cricket will sing.
You will like his songs.

If a stranger invites you
through the screen,
into this dream village

where the voices of animals
invite you to stroke their soft fur
then warm your hands

in their mouths,
run home.
If nothing in the theater

threatens you,
know, at least, that you will
leave a changed girl.

You will walk home down
Saginaw Street with a little piece
of yourself dissolving

in the belly of that whale.
In Stromboli's cage another bit
will wait to sing and dance

for strange men
and women and children
who were never warned

that your orphan song
will forever change them.
I will be listening.

Though I will like your song
and wish you the best,
I will not be able to save you.

Country Western and the Dead

I can't imagine the decomposing.
They lift from this life

instead and earn their sequins,

becoming Nashville
superstars, turning

(not in their graves
but in their songs,)
completing their sequence.

Long white robes and riversides.

My great-uncle, Walter Colpus
(I never met him)

welcomes the yearling
that I hit with my car last week,

his mandolin playing
and showmanship

only hinted at
in this life.

And the young deer's coat
slowly turns to white polyester,

its speckles to musical clefs
its eyes to giant rhinestones.

There will be no further initiations,
only the baby bottle of cream
and my mother's lap as a pillow.

The bleaching of the hymnal page.

The rosin that survives the bow.

Chief Pontiac Suffers Insomnia

If you love me, pray for sleep.
Pray that I will not spend

yet another night in my backyard
chained to consciousness

as a new moon plays
hard-to-get with the Dutch elm,

and the garden gnomes
all come around with gold coins

for instant winners, mistaking me
for an all-night Mobil Station.

That big red Pegasus
will not leave me alone.

It's nearly 4:00 a.m. again,
and the whir of a weathered motor

pumps water down the tiered slate
of my rock garden.

This is where I wait for sleep.
This is my landscaped hair shirt.

Oh, let the bed forgive me
of whatever I've done wrong.

I'll make a deal.
I'll confess to anything.

I'll sign whatever treaty sleep
would have me sign,

then say goodnight
to the curtained moon and the Persian

stonecress flanking the small
man-made waterfall that collects itself

where the little bronze statue
of John F. Kennedy wades

ankle-deep, untroubled
by the threat of yet another sunrise.

If J.F.K. knows what's wrong with me,
he's keeping it under his metallic lapel.

Zorro's Daughter

Still, the night disintegrates
lovely in its lesser attributes:

the wind, the lack of definition,
overfed raccoon and tactless moth

offering its body up to something
other than flame.

                    We ourselves
are famous for even less.

Though the best lives have all been lived,

we make the rent and have enough

left over for flat champagne in a paper cup.

She touches me

with her hand

and then the letter "z."

Pastoral with Chainsaw

1.

It was after the fall of Saddam Hussein,
during the hockey playoffs.

I'd never learned when not to ask,
How was your day?

We were renting a beat-up bungalow
thirty miles north of the university,
where our neighbors did all of their yard work
in the nude.

Potentially nice.
Two bodies toned and tanned.

Gently pressing tulip bulbs
into the soil.

But these two spent their Sunday mornings
cutting down trees with chain saws.

Naked.

2.

Humans were never meant to evolve.
That's how her day had been.

But ape's dark mutation allowed us to meet.

She understood evil better than I.
She understood evil better than me.

She knew my case for human evolution
was a selfish one.

Extrapolated from kisses
and obscure Japanese horror films.

3.

Each Sunday morning the neighbors
ripped through our dreams.
A perfect parody of Adam and Eve.

From our windows, we watched
stray bits of the landscape
stick to their sweaty bodies.

We watched the clearing expand
into an amphitheater
where the Cro-Mags sang:

if this be love,
if this be love,
if this be love.

Lullaby

If there is nothing
behind the music and music
behind the nothing and nothing
and so on,

then at least the baby's breathing.
Like an agitated bratwurst
or an old man's ear.
He needs no dream

because the memory of cell
division still counts off in his head.
If he's nearly beside himself,
it's because he's not there yet.

If he screams we wipe him dry.
The nights are getting bigger.
Sometimes I wish I had a telescope
mounted on my rocking chair,

an open window
and some general sense
of Aldebaran's whereabouts.
The three of us will never be big enough.

Having rearranged ourselves –
black egg, white semen –
we have seen that civilization,
if nothing else, is singing

to assure its young
that between our best efforts
and the universal eyelid, there's a yellow
bellied red bird, a plum tree and a bear.

Trains at Impossible Angles

East and west of everything
but himself, the passenger
can only sleep

or imagine things
as they may have been:
Detroit shovels coal

through the night
only to stay warm enough
to shovel coal again

when the church bells ring.
Tomorrow trapped in a yesterday.
Chicago has locked

its apartment doors
and unbuckled its icy shoes.
The rest of the world

waits for the quiet
return of something that never was.
It's impossible

to know,
            as the snow

starts to fall,
                        and Salvation

Army bands all over
the city call it quits,
what he might

have actually seen
from the window,
                    pulling away

from what he may have missed.

Epitaph

He never knew exactly
what the poets meant when they wanted
to stroke the fur of "animals
that lived in other animals."

He had nothing for the psychoanalyst.
That ancient confessional couch,
its springs broken by human misery,
its upholstery stained by human grease,
never held him in its arms.

He married and fathered two children
who confused him from time to time.

He enjoyed talk radio
while driving in his car.

Once in a required junior college
course in philosophy,
he became annoyed with Zeno's
motion paradox:

The professor might need to travel
in nothing but ever decreasing
half distances toward her sketchy destination,
but he'd simply step over the goal line.

If this is his epitaph,
he'd never have recognized it as such.

If he is in the cold, cold ground,
be comforted, my passionate ones,
that it's not quite as cold to him.

Toy Boat

We've been talking all night
about the night and how the night
leaves us just enough to say,
like a wooden ship departing,
its few visible moonlit lines
inseparable from what it is.

We've been practicing at love
and philosophy with nothing more
than the miniatures that night
has whittled to fit our hands.
We have said "night" and said "love"
and said "like a wooden ship departing."

Otherwise Engaged Literature and Arts Journal	"Country Western and the Dead"
Poetry Northwest	"A City of Hats"
The Puritan	"Mr. and Mrs. Tattoo"
Qu	"Chief Pontiac Answers Lord Jeffery"
Rogue Poetry	"Black Coffee"
Rougarou	"Our Finest Hour"
Route Nine	"Chief Pontiac Suffers Insomnia"
Slant	"Famous Succubus Trading Cards"
Steam Ticket	"As Her Children Debate"
Stickman Review	"Chief Pontiac Digs His Fortress"
The Thing Itself	"Breakfast Meditation"
Transcendence	"Instead of Discussing Marriage"
When In Drought	"Toy Boat"

www.ingramcontent.com/pod-product-compliance
Lightning Source LLC
Chambersburg PA
CBHW022201160726
48282CB00024B/281
* 9 7 8 9 3 9 5 2 2 4 1 4 7 *